Travis the T-Rex was angry. The rage inside his body grew and grew until it felt like his head would explode. Travis lashed out with his giant right foot, kicking Clayton Clubtail in the shins. Travis then turned around and stomped home. It wasn't a very good way to finish the school week.

1

The next Monday, Travis spent his lunch hour with his teacher Mrs Duckbill.

'It's normal to get angry from time to time Travis,' explained Mrs Duckbill.
'The problem is when you can't control your anger and you hurt someone or something.'

'I'm sorry Mrs Duckbill,' said Travis.
'It's not me that you need to apologise to Travis. Now, let's begin our exercises.'

Mrs Duckbill taught Travis to go to his *happy place*. Whenever he felt his anger rising, Travis could close his eyes and imagine that he was in a calm place. Travis took a deep breath and, in his mind, he pretended to be at the beach.

Travis loved sand castles and he imagined making a tall tower out of the wet sand. He could hear the waves crashing onto the beach and as he breathed, he thought about the tide coming in and out. Travis could taste the salty air and feel the cool breeze on his scales. He opened his eyes. 'That feels better,' said Travis.

Next, Mrs Duckbill taught Travis to be an iceberg.

'Clench your fists,' said Mrs Duckbill.
'Now, scrunch up your face.
Squeeze every muscle in your chest and arms. Squeeze every muscle in your legs and toes. Squeeze until your whole body feels tight.'

Travis scrunched and squeezed until he felt as hard as a block of ice.

'Now relax,' said Mrs Duckbill, 'and feel yourself slowly melt into a warm puddle of water.'

Travis relaxed and felt the anger drain out of his body.

'That feels better,' said Travis.

On Tuesday, Travis pretended he was a flat tyre.

'When you feel angry Travis, you need to stay calm. Now, slowly pump up your tyre,' said Mrs Duckbill.

Travis took a deep breath and filled his tyre with air. With each breath in and out, the tyre slowly inflated.

Travis kept breathing in and out slowly until his tyre was full of air. As he breathed out for the last time, he let all of the air out of the tyre. As the air escaped, the anger from his body flowed with it.

'That feels better,' said Travis.

On Wednesday, Travis practised his counting.

'When you get angry,' said Mrs Duckbill, 'breathe in and slowly count to ten in your head. Tell yourself to calm down and then take control of your decision.'
Travis breathed in and slowly counted in his head.

'1…2…3…4…5…6…7…8…9…10.'

He then breathed out slowly.

'That feels better,' said Travis.

On Thursday, Travis was angry. It was lunchtime and no one would play with him. Travis found a quiet place where he could be alone.

He thought about his happy place and calmed himself down. Travis then went to find Mrs Duckbill to tell her how he felt.

'You have a reputation Travis,' explained Mrs Duckbill. 'Many of the other children are scared to play with you in case you lose your temper.'

'How do I lose my reputation?' asked Travis.

'You can't lose a reputation Travis but you can change one,' said Mrs Duckbill.

On Friday, the rage inside Travis' body grew and grew until it felt like his head would explode. He was in the playground, facing Clayton Clubtail and Ellie Saurus. Ellie Saurus was laughing and making fun of Travis' tiny arms.

Travis took a deep breath and counted to ten. As he breathed out, he still felt like hitting Ellie and showing her how strong his little arms were. He tried to put his hands in his pockets but he couldn't reach them. His arms were so short that he couldn't even put his hands behind his back.

Travis breathed in again and made a decision. He pressed his hands firmly together and pushed. As he pushed he squeezed his strong arm muscles and clenched his teeth. Then he slowly relaxed his arms until he felt his anger drain away. Travis then turned to Ellie and looked her in the eyes.

'Stop Ellie!' said Travis. 'I don't like it when you tease me.' Travis then turned to face Clayton Clubtail. 'Clayton, I apologise for kicking you last week. That was wrong of me and I am very sorry for hurting you. It won't happen again.' Travis the T-Rex then turned and walked away.

'Wait up Travis!' called Clayton.
'How about a game of handball?'

'That would be great,' said Travis.
Travis and Clayton headed off together
toward the handball courts. After a few
steps, Travis turned around to look at Ellie
who was now standing all alone.

'You're welcome to join us Ellie,'
Travis said with a smile.

Activities

Look at the angry T-Rex and explain to everyone what is making this T-Rex so angry.

Look at the images of the happy T-Rex and explain to everyone what is making this T-Rex so happy.

Look at the following images and explain to everyone what are your feelings when you see this. Can you explain how you can change?

Look at the following images and explain to everyone what are your feelings when you see this. Can you explain how you can change?